Miracles Do Happen!

by Retha Boyd

Published by:
Vicktory Center Ministries, Inc.
662-323-3740
Starkville, MS

Cover Art by:
Michael Strobel

Contents

V

Acknowledgements

I gratefully acknowledge my husband, Michael T. Boyd, pastor of Victory Center Church, for his support, typing skills and patience as he helped to make the publishing of this book possible. Thank you for your tireless energy, devotion and labor of love. You are my friend and constant companion, thank you for helping me to tell my story. Continue to be steadfast and unmovable, always abounding in the work of the Lord, for as much as you know, your labor is not in vain in the Lord, remember, you have the victory.

Thank you Dr. Barbara Pitts for allowing God to use you to prophesy the writing of this book before the thought was even conceived in my mind. May God ever bless your powerful ministry.

Preface

The body of Christ has for many years recognized the fact that miracles "can" happen, but I propose to you the fact that miracles "do" happen, and more often than many of us recognize. The supernatural power of God is at work all around us everyday. Angels witness the miraculous occurrence of heavens visitation upon the lives of mortal men and are left with the question "why" forever lingering on their lips. In Psalms 8:4 the angels pose the question "what is man, that thou art mindful of him? And the Son of man that thou visitest him? For thou hast made him a little lower than the angels, and hast crowned him with glory and honor." When David understood just what God had done for us mere mortals he cried, " O Lord our Lord, how excellent is thy name in all the earth!

I am not a pastor, prophetess nor great evangelist, I have no degree nor popularity, I'm just a servant, yet God has allowed me the privilege to glimpse into some of his glorious miracles and afforded me this opportunity to share these experiences. I'm not writing this book to convince either a skeptic or cynical person of anything. The experiences I'm sharing are too sacred to be put under a microscope to be dissected in the hope that someone will come away believing, I'm writing to make a definitive statement that...
"MIRACLES DO HAPPEN!"

Miracles Do Happen!

Chapter One

Struggling To Find My Way

I was born in a little town called Buckingham, Virginia. I was raised by my grandparents from the time I was three weeks old and grew up with an older brother, aunt and uncle. I was the youngest and the heart of my grandfather. He died in 1988 and "mama" my grandmother, went to be with the Lord in 1997. At the age of thirteen I left Buckingham and went to live in Washington D. C. with my mother, a younger brother and sister. We attended a church called Tyson Temple First Born Church of the Living God. From the street you could hear the sound of people rejoicing, the tinkling of cymbals and singing, not well blended operatic voices, but glorious sounds of praise that came straight from the heart. I'll never forget the first time I walked into that church. As we entered the building my mother hurried to take her seat, but I stood there frozen for a moment as I felt the sincerity of their praise and worship. They played drums, tambourines and old fashioned wash boards, this was different from anything I had ever experienced in my previous church. The congregation was caught up in praise and worship. An old church mother, whom I later learned was Mother Bishop, walked the aisles with a cane in her hand singing "If I don't wake up in the morning, everything will be alright." There was a glow in her eyes and a peace on her face that said she wasn't worried about tomorrow, that everything was all right. The service was wonderful and I left excited. From that night on, anytime my mother said she was going to church, no problem, I was ready!

One afternoon I went outside to play on the playground. All the swings were broken and hung suspended by one chain. I climbed aboard and stood with one foot on either side of the black rubber seat. To my surprise a boy ran up behind me and pushed the swing. My feet slipped and I fell on to the hard rubber seat. I can still recall the pain that went through my pelvic area. The boy was scared and ran off. I laid on the ground wondering how I was going to get back home; walking was only a brief thought. I crawled until I reached the door of my apartment. I was then taken to the hospital and admitted.

The doctors said that I had internal bleeding and may never be able to conceive because of the damage I'd done internally, but God had other plans. Little did I know that this was a prelude to the miraculous healing power of God that I would see in the years to come. I recovered without ever having an operation and was released from the hospital a week later. I knew that God was in that hospital. I felt his love and kindness through the doctors and nurses that attended me. I never had one frightening moment during my stay there. Though I had not personally received Him, God was with me. As I raced the corridors in my wheel chair, God worked a miracle in my body, I was healed!

I saw the tender mercies of God through the faces of the nurses and staff members who went beyond the call of duty and sat with me through the nights.

Jeremiah 30:17 says "I will restore health unto thee, and heal thee of all thy wounds." My health was restored and my wounds were healed.

Six years later I gave birth to twin girls. Two years after that I had another baby girl. God touched my life with loving kindness and what I'd felt all along was true, He was there, Praise God, Miracles Do Happen!

Chapter Two

Going Back

The following year I returned to Buckingham, Virginia to more familiar surroundings. At home I was carefree with no obligations or commitments. Everything was fine for awhile but soon I began to miss the service I'd enjoyed at Tyson Temple First Born Church of the Living God. I couldn't forget the songs, the preaching, and the music that had so drawn me to that church. I had tasted and found that the Lord was good. He had satisfied my mouth with good things! I was hungry for more of the same.

God told David in Psalms 32:8, "I will instruct thee and teach thee in the way which thou shalt go. I will guide thee with mine eye." I felt a tugging in my spirit that I couldn't explain. The memories flooded my mind every day and finally I told mama, my grandmother who raised me since I was three weeks old that I had to go back. It hurt mama to know that once again I would be leaving and this time for good, but there was a longing in my soul that had to be satisfied. I had heard John 10: 3-4 read many times, saying the sheep hear his voice and he calleth his own sheep by name, and leadeth them out, and when he putteth forth his own sheep, he goeth before them, and the sheep follow him, for they know his voice. I didn't know about predestination then, I didn't know about the wisdom of Solomon and how he said that to every thing there is a season, and a time for every purpose under the heavens. God had his purpose and this was my time to go back, to be led in a path that would change my life forever, but I had absolutely nothing to do with it. My destiny was in God's hands. It was important to be in the right place at the right time. Everyone's place and time is different and if you're out of place, you can easily miss your time. I didn't understand why the unction was in me so strong to go back to Washington D.C., but now I know that the shepherd had called his sheep by name and was leading me to the place that I might be found in him. I was lost and needed to be found. We think that we find Jesus, but Jesus is never lost, it's us that need to be found. Everyone that comes to Him has his or her own place of discovery.

Nicodemus was found one day under the cover of darkness, Nathaniel was coming out from under a fig tree, the Ethiopian eunuch was going down to Jerusalem, Saul was coming near Damascus and I was coming up from Buckingham.

The decision to go back to Washington D.C. was not an easy one, but I knew it was the best one. God was with me through some difficult times in my early years. If it hadn't been for the Lord, I know I wouldn't be here today to tell my story. I praise God, He was there. Though I hadn't acknowledged the Lord as my savior I was always conscious of the fact that He was there watching over me. During my early teens I was heading for trouble but the Lord preserved me during a time when I felt desperate for love and acceptance. Sometimes the Lord will bring us through trouble and other times He keeps us "from" trouble. Paul said in 2 Timothy 4:18 the Lord shall deliver me from every evil work, and will preserve me unto His heavenly kingdom, to whom be glory forever and ever. Perhaps God knew had I gotten into trouble, I wouldn't have been able to resist the temptation and come out, so He kept me "from" trouble.

God preserved me from every evil work and even from my youth, God counted me into His heavenly kingdom, and though I hadn't arrived yet, He counted me as already present.

Chapter Three

The Bus That Wouldn't Stop

School had been dismissed several times because of bomb threats, but that was o.k. with me, for all it meant to me was that we missed a couple of classes. One Friday morning it was no longer O.K.; they found a bomb in the locker next to mine and the reality of death hit home. I knew that if I died, I would be eternally separated from Jesus, and though I didn't really know Him, the thought was more than I could bear. I'd heard the story of the rich man and the beggar Lazarus and how they both died and Lazarus went to Abraham's bosom and was comforted, but the rich man was tormented in the flames. A great gulf was fixed so that neither could cross over. If I died now, I would be lost forever; I'd be tormented in the flames.

I remembered the dream I'd had several nights before that haunted me like a bad nightmare. In my dream I got on the bus and the driver had a bald head and a broad smile on his face. He watched in the mirror and waited as I took my seat. After a moment I realized I was going the wrong direction and pulled the bell to get off. The driver wouldn't stop. I stood up and said, "Stop the bus, I need to get off, I'm going the wrong way." I looked at the driver and he had changed to this mean evil creature with red eyes, he wasn't smiling anymore. All the people began to chant over and over again, "You're going the wrong way. You're going the wrong way." In my dream I never got off the bus, but I knew in life I had to get off and this was my stop. I wonder today how many are still going the wrong way and you hear it over and over again, "You're going the wrong way." Don't miss your stop, if you miss it you may never get off. Don't ride this bus to your destruction, its going the wrong way, rise up and ring the bell. Get desperate, your eternal soul is at stake. You're going the wrong way! Jesus foreknew that we would arrive at the crossroads of making a decision and He gave specific instructions saying " Enter ye in at the strait gate." The gate is so straight till no crooked or perverse thing can enter in. The way is so narrow that it requires much sacrifice. Paul strengthened our hearts by letting us know that when he added it all up, he reckoned that the sufferings of this present world are not worthy to be compared to the glory that shall be revealed in us. So though we enter in through self-denial and with much tribulation, the sacrifice is well worth the reward. We endure the cross for the joy that is set before us even as our elder brother Jesus did. We enter in at the strait gate to be counted as one of the few that find it, BUT YOU'VE GOT TO GET OFF THE BUS!

There are always those that will stay on the bus for the ride, they get caught up in the motion and just ride to the end of the line. They wake up too late and find they're lost and their transfer has run out. Some never rise to ring the bell to say , "That's far enough, I'm getting off." In my dream the bus wouldn't stop, but then, it was only a dream, I woke up! Some never wake up, they keep on riding the bus that's going the wrong way until they're lost… eternally lost. No matter how loud they scream or how much they repent, they'll forever know they stayed on the bus that wouldn't stop! I made the decision to give my life to Jesus. I knew he could do more with it than I could. I trusted Jesus to be my Lord and Saviour, but that was only the beginning. I knew that if I was to stay saved I needed power, I needed the Holy Ghost. A revival was being held at Tyson Temple and the late Bishop Potter was there running the meeting. In those days we went to the altar and got on our knees and clapped our hands and called Jesus. We called Him long, loud and hard, we did whatever the church mothers told us to do because we wanted Him that bad. James Steadman, Rita Cunningham and I were on the altar to receive the Holy Ghost. James came through first, he later became pastor of Tyson Temple. I, however, was left on the altar. It was Friday and I told the church that I couldn't leave till I received the Holy Ghost, I was scared to leave there without Him. We need more people to become scared. People don't fear or revere anything or anyone anymore, but I was scared to live in this world any longer without the Holy Ghost. Bishop Potter asked me several questions about whether I believed I was justified by faith and sanctified from sin, neither of which I had a clue about. I was 15.

The bishop took time and taught me about faith in the Son of God and what his dying did for me. He told me how Jesus had washed my sins away with His blood and in simple language that the Holy Ghost would help me to keep the faith I had in Him. He was my keeper; I got the picture then! The service dismissed but the saints didn't leave me, they stayed and saw me through. I don't know how long I stayed on the altar, but it seemed like only moments. I felt my body get light, I fell backwards from my knees and then it happened! I heard a language I had never learned come forth out of my mouth, I was speaking in another tongue, and it was Pentecost for me! When the disciples were assembled together in the upper room, they were all filled with the Holy Ghost and began to speak with other tongues as the spirit gave them the utterance. That's what I had, a Holy Ghost utterance! Every believer ought to have one! In my dream the bus wouldn't stop, but praise God, I woke up, got off the bus, went through the gate called strait, and got the Holy Ghost!

Chapter Four

The Strong Arm of God

At sixteen years old I had graduated from high school and was living in my own apartment, fully furnished with the furniture I had bought while working half days during my senior year. One night I was preparing to go to bed and all of the lights went out. I didn't have any candles or flashlight; I was in complete darkness. I was fumbling around for a few minutes hoping to find a match, anything so I could see. Then suddenly there was a knock on the door, thinking it was the electrician to turn on the power, I opened the door to my basement apartment. A man immediately began to force his way inside.

I've never been as afraid as I was then. Physically I was no match against this man, I was only 95 pounds but instinctively I found myself grabbing him below, I kneed him where it hurts a man most. I saw this look in his eyes as he doubled over in pain; it surprised me as much as it did him. As he stooped and doubled over in pain, I pushed the door forcing him backwards and out the door. I later learned that the electric box was on the outside of my basement apartment and the switch had been pulled putting me in total darkness.

I learned a valuable lesson about opening the door without knowing who it is. I was set up for a fall but God had his angels encamped round about me and gave His angels charge over me that I didn't become a victim of such a horrible crime. The strong arm of God saved me. In my weakness He was my strength. David called him the saving strength of his anointed. I hadn't been anointed yet, but I was blessed. Satan meant it for a tragedy, but God enabled me to triumph. I know that I received a miracle that night, I had no strength to fight this battle; this battle belonged to the Lord. The strong arm of the Lord fought for me and delivered me from the hand of the enemy. God was my refuge and my strength, His strong arm gave me the victory. In my weakness, He gave me a miracle of strength.

Chapter Five

A Most Unusual Delivery

Several years later I got married and became pregnant with babies doctors thought I'd never have. God had completely healed my body and brought about conception. Not only was I pregnant, but expecting twins! Some people say it's double the trouble, but for me it was double the blessing! During my second trimester I was told that there would be complications if I tried to have natural birth. I was told I could die trying to give birth or the babies could die trying to be born. At the first sign of labor I was to call my doctor and go immediately to the hospital.

I was given a sealed envelope that I was to take with me; it explained my condition in case there was an emergency. No one could have anticipated the emergency that awaited us, but God had everything in control. I was now in my ninth month and everything had gone well except for a few fainting spells.

It was March 10, 1973 around 3:00 a.m. when the first pains began. I called my doctor but he said it was too early for the babies to arrive and that I should wait awhile before going to the hospital. I was told that first babies never come on time and since I was having a cesarean section I had time. I didn't understand because he had previously stressed the urgency of getting to the hospital before I went into hard labor. Thirty minutes had passed and I began to feel a baby's head pushing through. We got into the car and raced toward the hospital, running red lights and blowing the horn. The motorists were extremely courteous and pulled off the road and sometimes going through the lights themselves, clearing a path for us. At 9th and Pennsylvania Avenue in Washington D. C. we noticed a police cruiser behind us and another beside us. Everyone had been so kind, sensing an emergency situation was in progress and letting us pass, but the two cruisers were pursuing us. One cruiser sped ahead and quickly blocked us at an angle with his car. My now ex-husband had a quick decision, there was no way he could stop the car, he mashed his brakes and started skidding. It was either the police car or this huge steel lamppost. We hit the police cruiser. Had we hit the lamppost I believe that we would have been dead today. The driver's door was jammed and badly smashed, it wouldn't open. At the impact of the crash, I felt my baby being born; she laid there crying, completely visible except for her feet. The police began to interrogate my ex-husband, as he remained trapped inside the car. He managed to explain to an unidentified man that he needed help, I couldn't get out of the car and I'd just had the baby. The man got my door opened, picked me up and carried me to the rear of the other police cruiser that had been following us. An ambulance arrived; the attendant threw a blanket over the police cruiser window to cover me from the people that had begun to gather around.

The paramedic then cut the umbilical cord and Shontel Colette was born at 5:20AM. The unidentified man comforted me and rode with me in the patrol car to the hospital. I never found out his name but I will never forget his kindness. When I arrived at George Washington University Hospital I was very concerned about my first child because we were separated and I hadn't received any reports concerning her condition. She had remained in the front seat during the ride to the hospital. I tried to explain to the nurses upon my arrival that I was having another baby but they kept telling me to rest.

They said I'd had my baby and the physicians were examining her. They didn't know that I was carrying twins. When they finally opened the manila envelope I was carrying explaining my need for a cesarean, to everyone's surprise there were only blank sheets of paper sealed inside the envelope. I never arrived at Columbia hospital where I was scheduled to deliver my babies. A few minutes later I began to feel more pains. They lasted for about twenty minutes and then my second baby, Daenel Arkese was born. I'll never forget that day. I arrived at the hospital in the back of the police car and my now ex-husband arrived in the ambulance, he was fine, just needed a ride! His 1972 Datsun was totaled and $800.00 damage was done to the patrol car, a 1971 Plymouth. The story was on the front page of the Washington Post on March 10-14 in 1973. I kept these news articles all these years so that my children could read the story of their births.

Now they are able to pass the story on to their children. I still have a copy of the original story today after twenty- six years and it still amazes me how everyone came through by the grace of God. Anything could have gone differently at any sequence of the events and changed all of our lives, but I'm grateful to God that He spared our lives and blessed us to be able to tell about it twenty-six years later. I thank God for my children, they are miracles from God, and it was a most unusual delivery!

Chapter Six

God Healed My Babies

Hours after my youngest twin was born, she began to experience breathing difficulties. She was also having problems keeping her formula down. She was premature and her lungs weren't fully developed. She would lie in her bed and stop breathing. She had to be watched around the clock so we were advised to leave her at the hospital.

Meanwhile, the oldest twin was thriving and doing fine, but because she was born outside the hospital under a non-sterile environment she was placed in isolation. For the first two days I was not able to hold my first born. She rode in the front seat of the police car and was taken into the immediate care of the doctors and nurses. Then she was placed in isolation. I wanted to hold her so bad and let her know how much I loved her and had waited for her and her sister to arrive. I could only stare through the window and pray that everything would be all right.

I continued to hold and feed my youngest daughter; she looked just like me except for her eyes; she had her grandmothers' eyes on her fathers' side. She was so small that I could hold her in one hand. Her lungs still weren't functioning properly and she was being placed on a pillow to sleep, hoping the elevation would help. On the third day I was reunited with my oldest daughter Shontel. I finally had the opportunity to hold her for the first time since our admittance into the hospital. Upon my discharge the doctors allowed me to take Shontel, my oldest baby, home. Daenel, my youngest daughter had to stay longer to be monitored by the nurses to ensure that her lungs would develop a little more, and provide her emergency service if needed. I was glad to be going home but sad to leave my other daughter behind but I knew I couldn't risk taking her home at this time. She stayed in the hospital another week and we received the call to come get her. She was still having a problem digesting formula but was taking in enough to gain weight. Her lungs were functioning better but she still had to be watched constantly as she laid on her back on a pillow. The second night she was home I woke up to the sound of gurgling noises. I looked over in the crib and my baby was struggling to breathe. Her body was stiff and she'd turned blue, I had to act fast, there was no time to panic. The doctor had instructed me to pick her up by her feet, turn her upside down and give two sharp pats between her shoulder blades, stop for two counts and repeat the process. I did and it worked; she began to breathe. Everyday I was grateful to have my baby alive. I can't tell you how many times during those first six months of her life I sat by her bed in a chair watching her sleep and catching her just in time as she fought to get air into her lungs. I know it was the Lord that saw us through those first six months of her life. Sometimes I'd be asleep and wouldn't hear anything, but God would allow me to wake up just in time. Getting a babysitter was out of the question during those early months. I couldn't afford to leave them for appointments or anything else. I purchased a back harness and when I went shopping, I carried them with me, one in my arms and the other on my back.

Finally, when she was about six months old she began to sleep through the night without anymore breathing difficulties. It had been a long and exhaustive six months, but with much prayer we made it through! Glory to God! But just when we think we have stood all we can stand, we find that we have to stand some more. Romans 14:4b talks about God's divine support, saying He shall be holden or held up, for God is able to make him stand. I know it was the Lord that gave me strength to stand through those many sleepless nights and when I'd done all to stand, I yet had to stand therefore… but the good news is that God is faithful, even when we're unfaithful, and will not suffer us to be tempted above that which we are able. God knows the full measure of every man's endurance; he knows just how much we can bear. He allows our test to come up to our strength, but not beyond our strength. We must be able through the grace of God to bear it.

When Daenel was about ten months old she began to have seizures. She had violent seizures that contorted her little body and jerked her with such force that it was sometimes difficult to hold her. Her temperature would become elevated if she had a cold and I found myself rushing her back and forth to the hospital. Sometimes she would seize for no apparent reason. There were times when she would be sitting in a shopping cart in a store and go into a seizure. When she was three she had a grand mal seizure, it caused her to have a temporary memory lapse. I was told if it didn't reverse in twenty-four hours it could be permanent. She was on medication every four hours, even if she was asleep I had to wake her to give her the medication. Her temperature would go from 103 to 106 degrees nearing the point of brain damage as she continued to convulse. I had dedicated my babies to God when they were born and I realized that they were in his hands. God was so merciful and brought her back time and time again. It wasn't the doctors, it wasn't the medication, it was a miracle from God! Satan sought to steal, kill, and destroy. But God kept her alive. I stood helpless as

I saw my child go through painful spinal taps. She laid limp with her eyes opened and not making a sound. Other times she screamed so loud as the needle entered her spine that I couldn't stand it; I had to leave the hospital floor. It was hard to see my baby tied down to the bed so she wouldn't hurt herself as her body convulsed out of control. The medicines were helping to keep some of her seizures under control but by the time she was three they no longer had the same effect. She was unable to sleep at night and was developing a case of hyperactivity. I would hear her at 3:00 and 4:00 a.m. hitting toys on the walls. The congregation at my church continued to pray with me and believe God that she would be healed. God was our only hope. I'd heard Isaiah 53:5 "With his stripes we are healed" quoted many times during our services. God said that we "are" (present tense) healed. Even though she was convulsing, according to faith in the word of God, she was healed. We didn't have to believe "He will heal." When He says you are healed, right now, it's done! Glory be to God! My baby was healed! We began to accept this that God had imparted to our spirits. Despite what we see or feel, the word of God is true. Jesus had taken the stripes for our healing that we wouldn't be defeated by sickness. We received it, and just as anyone does with good manners, we began to thank God for her healing. The just live by faith, not by sight, sight can blind you. Many have lost their blessing because of what they see. What you see can weaken your faith. Sometimes we have to close our eyes and just believe God! Hallelujah! Soon the seizures became fewer and fewer. I had already taken her off the medication and put her on "God!" And bless his name, He was working! My daughter is healed, set free to the glory of God! Faith is the substance; the reality of the things believed for, the evidence, the proof of the things that are not seen. If you have to see it to believe it, then where is faith? Faith says I believe it even though I can't see it. I believe it and it's done! Praise God!

Two years after the twins were born I had another daughter. She also began to suffer with seizures, but I knew what worked now! What God had done for one, surely he would do for the other. Job 22:28 says, "Thou shalt decree a thing and it shall be established unto thee." We decreed healing and rebuked that infirmity in Jesus name. We read everything on healing back to God. We found it in the scripture and rehearsed his word in His ears. Proverbs 4:22 says, "His word is life unto those that find them and health to all their flesh." My baby needed both, and again we began to celebrate in advance for what God had done. I mean celebrate from the heart, knowing, not hoping, but knowing it's done. God heard the celebration! He heard us clapping and thanking him for what He had done... And he did it! God gave us a healing miracle. God healed my babies!

Chapter Seven

I Saw His Goodness

In 1975 my now ex-husband and I had separated and I had nowhere to go. I remembered that my mother's house was under construction and she had moved out because the house was unlivable. When you have nowhere to live, you live where you can. I took the canned food I had and my girls and I stayed in this house that was being renovated for several days. There was a full crew working in the house but no one bothered us. The ceiling was exposed and some of the floor was gone, but I found a place to lay my twins and I leaned against the wall and slept. We ate pork 'n' beans, Vienna sausages, and crackers. We couldn't get near the kitchen, but that was o.k. because I didn't have anything to cook anyway. I had already used the food that my mother had given me from her freezer.

I've never been prouder of my girls, they

never complained. They trusted me to do the very best for them and I trusted God to do what was best for us. Even without a place to go and barely enough food to eat, I knew somehow we would be all right. I had a promise through the mouth of David that God would provide. David said in Psalms 37:25 "I have been young and now am old, yet have I not seen the righteous forsaken, nor his seed begging bread." I 'm a seed of Abraham and have a right to the children's bread. Just because I ate beans out of a can didn't mean God loved me any less, for many are the afflictions of the righteous, but the Lord delivereth him out of them all. There was deliverance for me; I just didn't know when or where. One of my relatives told me I could stay with them but a couple of days later I was told I had to leave and my bags had already been packed. I didn't have anywhere to go so I said take me to the church. When you don't know where to go, go to church, there's always a blessing at God's house. My bag was put down on the walkway and I really didn't know what to do. I had two small children and no place to call my own. I wanted to break down and cry but I was afraid that if I started I wouldn't be able to stop. Surely God would make a way somehow.

Just like God did with Abraham, he had a ram in the bush. One of my friends was going out of town; she gave me the keys to her apartment for a week. I know it was the goodness of Jesus, only He knew how much I needed Him. Jesus said "I will never leave you nor forsake you, lo, I am with you always even to the end of the world." We had a shower, a clean bed and food... the righteous would not be forsaken, God was a present help in my time of trouble. The righteous run unto Him and are saved until they're safe!

The Lord is the strength of my life, and in Him there is no weakness at all! David said in Psalms 27:13 I had fainted, unless I had believed to see the goodness of the Lord in the land of the living.

I've seen the goodness of the Lord while I live, and I know the faithfulness of His word. His word is like a nail fastened in a sure place. The weight of the world can be hung upon it but it shall not be moved because it's anchored. The goodness of God is a sure foundation, built upon this promise, that the Lord know them that are His.

We are called according to His purpose that was predestined from the foundation of the world. We know His thoughts concerning us that they are good. Praise God, I saw His goodness!

Chapter Eight

In The Company Of An Angel

In 1976 I decided to leave Washington, D.C. and try to work at our troubled marriage. My now ex-husband was stationed in El Paso, Texas. He asked the girls and I to come. The trip would take two days. Traveling with two 3-year-olds and a five-month-old baby would not be easy. I knew I would need the Lord, but never did I think He would come like He did! I was standing in line waiting to board the bus when an elderly woman came up and asked how far I was going, I said, "To El Paso," and she said "Good, we can travel together." I was relieved that I didn't have to travel alone and being with this elderly woman somehow made me feel safe. I had hoped that no one would talk to me during this trip and was prepared to be on my own, but for some reason I immediately welcomed the company of this elderly lady.

We boarded the bus and rode into the night.

When I woke up it was light outside. We had stopped at a little café and I wanted to get off and get something hot to drink but the children were lying across me asleep. I didn't want to wake them so I decided to just sit still. A few moments later my new found friend returned carrying two cups of hot chocolate, just what I wanted! Praise God! I was so grateful she was there.

When we finally arrived in El Paso I couldn't wait for my now ex- husband to meet her. I saw him coming and turned to greet him and started to introduce him to her. I wanted to share with him what a help she had been, but, she was gone. I couldn't believe she could have left that quick. I had only turned for a moment and she was gone. She was too old to be running, where did she go? I looked around but couldn't find her. Maybe someone had seen her leave; she couldn't have gotten far. I never had a chance to thank her. I had to find her. I asked one of the men that had been sitting across from us on the bus, but he said there wasn't anyone there. How could he not see this woman? He said it had only been the children and

I sitting there. What was wrong with him? She had been with me for two days and now she had simply vanished and he never saw her! I asked the man standing beside me while I was talking to her, he said "I saw you talking to yourself but there wasn't anyone with you." I thought perhaps it was just the men who had gone crazy so I asked a young woman that I knew had seen us as we passed her coming in, but again, the same reply, "there wasn't anyone with you." I couldn't understand it, for two days I'd been with this elderly woman with the kind face that made me feel so safe, she brought me hot chocolate from the café. Could it be true? Was it an angel? Was I in the company of an angel unaware? Hebrews 13: 2b says some have entertained angels unaware. I know the bible is full of stories of angels that have ministered on our behalf from the Old Testament and throughout the New Testament. One day Gideon was threshing wheat and an angel came and sat under an oak tree and encouraged him saying the Lord is with thee, thou mighty man of valor. Manoah's wife was visited by an angel one day and told that though she was barren she would have a son. She conceived and bore a son and called his name Samson. Abram and Sarai entertained and fed angels. The prison doors were opened by angels for the Apostles. An angel caused Zacharias to become speechless until John was born.

Would God care enough to send an angel all the way from heaven to care for a lonely traveler with three babies? I'm the least of His servants, but I believe he would, and it has absolutely nothing to do with me. It's not how dedicated or faithful you are its not some reward for commitment or because of our righteousness, we have none, and all of our righteousness is as filthy rags. The good that's within us is the righteousness of Jesus Christ. If we were good then we'd have reason to boast because of the works of our flesh, but there is no good thing in the flesh. Paul said in Romans 9:16 that its not of him that willeth, nor of him that runneth, but God that showeth mercy. He has mercy on whom He will have mercy. And on whom He will, He hardeneth and no man can call Him unjust.

Who can say God, you shouldn't do this or you shouldn't do that, or do it this way? Who can counsel Him? He's the creator and we're His creation. David said we are the sheep of His pasture, we're privileged to enter into His gates with praise.

I'm so thankful to Him, I bless His name! If I could praise him from now until eternity, it would not suffice for all He's done for me. My Lord redeemed my soul and paid the price with His blood. I owe Him everything... Absolutely everything. In Him I live, I move and have my being. He's an awesome God!

Chapter Nine

I Could Not Deny Him

We were soon settled into our army quarters located on Victory Blvd. In El Paso, Texas, it was dry and dusty. Our quarters looked like little cabins all in a row. When it rained we got sandbags and packed them tightly around our houses to keep the water out. It was a new adventure, I didn't mind. All I wanted was a good church where I could praise the Lord, and I had plenty to praise him for! I found just the place, pastored by an elderly preacher. His wife was very loving and together they pointed the way to Christ. The pastor was often out of place and his assistant took charge of the service. People of all backgrounds attended this little church. There had been some controversy over receiving the Holy Ghost and it had been decided prior to my arrival that the church would not deal with the issue of the Holy Ghost. But the Holy Ghost had been such an important part of my life, I couldn't deny Him, I just couldn't! One of the deacons and His wife used to pick the girls and I up for church. He always looked straight ahead and never said very much. He strongly opposed any talk of the Holy Ghost, but his wife was hungry for Him. Together we read every scripture we could find on the Holy Ghost. She wasn't sure whether she needed Him or not. Just when I thought she was fully persuaded, someone would come along and sow a little seed of doubt and she'd be confused all over again. One Sunday morning after the message the altar call was made and I got right beside her. When she came through I didn't want to miss it! She was weeping and shaking, she was in the struggle of her life. She didn't know what to think, but I heard her say, "Lord, I don't know if I have to have the Holy Ghost or not, but if I do, fill me NOW!" The next thing I knew her lips began to tremble and she couldn't control it, she invited the Holy Ghost in and He took control. She started speaking just like they did on the day of Pentecost; other tongues came forth out of her mouth and I knew she was carrying on a conversation with heaven! She had the Holy Ghost and the Holy Ghost had her! She spoke for quite awhile as she kneeled on the altar and communed with heaven.

Now you would think that everybody would have been rejoicing and praising God. But no, that husband of hers was mad! We sat and waited for her to come around but she was still caught up in glory. She had waited for this for a long time and was determined to enjoy every moment! Her husband told the girls and I to get into the car. We got in thinking she would be out soon, but then he got in and started the engine. The locks went down and he pulled off. I said, "Wait, what about your wife? Where are we going?" We weren't going in the direction of my house. He never said a word, there was absolute silence. Finally, he pulled off onto a dirt road. I don't mind telling you I was scared, really scared. No one knew where we were and we were locked inside the car. He drove about a mile down the dirt road and stopped the car. He turned around in my face and reminded me how he had asked me to leave his wife alone; he had on several occasions. He told me to stay away from her. I quickly agreed. He turned around, started the engine and drove us home. I never told his wife and she never asked me about that day. I never rode with them again.

If there were other churches in the area, I didn't know it. I never visited any. Testimony service began the following Sunday and I stood to thank God for being so good to me. He had been good. I also thanked God for the Holy Ghost and how he comes to those that invite him in. I heard the bell ring and the devotional leader was ringing the bell drowning me out, I took my seat. I was told to abide by the rule or find another church. The next Sunday I returned and as I began testifying I heard the bell ringing again. I was politely asked to find another church. I didn't want to cry, but I felt the tears roll down my cheeks as I began to gather up my things. Suddenly there was a tap on my shoulder. An usher handed me a little yellow piece of paper with some words written on it. I blinked back the tears so I could read it. It said "smile, remember, they did Jesus worst, don't let it get you down, God loves you and so do I." I looked up wondering who had sent this little note that gave me strength when I needed it most. A young girl, about fourteen, waved from across the church, it was signed Fannie. I don't know where she is today, it has been over twenty years, but I kept that note all these years and it is still with me today. No wonder our Lord said a child shall lead them. I was about to leave when the door opened and a man came in dressed in overalls with a knapsack on his back, he had whiskers and long hair. There was something captivating about this old man as he came in and walked right down the middle aisle to the front of the church. He took charge of the service. All eyes were upon him as he began to tell how he was headed for Dallas, Texas, but the Lord told him to come to El Paso, to this church that he had never been to before. He said, "The Lord sent me here." (And I believed him!) Now of all the things he could have talked about, he started talking about the Holy Ghost. There was absolute silence in that room. He asked all those that "didn't" have the Holy Ghost to stand, people started standing all over the building. Then he said, "All those that want the Holy Ghost stay on your feet." People started sitting down as they rejected the precious Holy Ghost. There were only

46

about nine or ten still standing. He told them to come up to the front of the church and they lined up across the front facing him. But then, he looked in my direction and said, "Come here, stand beside me." Now remember, he had just come in, he had no idea about what had just happened. He'd never seen me before in his life. This man of God said, "come," and I stood right beside him. He said, "as I touch them, you move as I move." As he touched the first man, immediately he began to speak in tongues, I stood there overwhelmed by the awesome power of God, seeing how instantly this first man was filled with the Holy Ghost. I'd never seen anything like it! He had touched the second, the third and was moving toward the fourth when he saw that I was still at the first man. I heard him say "move when I move." He didn't have to say it again, I moved! On and on down the line each one received the Holy Ghost and began to speak in tongues as the Holy Ghost gave them the utterance.

Power fell from heaven that day as all that came forward to receive him went away full. Glory be to God! Praise God for men that are not too self-willed to be led by God. If he had kept to his agenda he would have been in Dallas, Texas and I would have missed my blessing along with all those that were miraculously filled that day. We don't always know how obedience will impact another person's life and that life will affect another and the blessing continues on.

I stayed at that little church for two more years. God broke a stronghold that day and the devil was defeated.

There are more things I "don't" know than what I "do" know, but one thing I do know is that Jesus meant it when He said, "Receive ye the Holy Ghost!" It's a gift, straight from Him to you. If you want it, open your mouth wide and take it. "You" do the speaking, God won't open up your mouth and force anything to come out, you must open your mouth, use your voice as the Holy Ghost does His part, His part is the utterance. Trust him, He'll do it! The Disciples spoke as the Holy Ghost gave them the utterance. You can't talk with your mouth shut, you've got to open your mouth and drink it in. Expect to speak in tongues, look forward to it. It will happen, you don't have to wait one more week, not one more month, not one more year, right now you can receive the Holy Ghost from God! Shut out everything and focus on Jesus, surrender your will and embrace His will. His will is that you be filled. Open your mouth and let your tongue go, you will feel the spirit move upon you. Stay there, continue to allow yourself to speak until a clear, free language comes and you hear yourself speak in another tongue. No one will have to tell you you're filled, you'll show the world you're filled. In the name of JESUS! RECEIVE the HOLY GHOST!

I almost didn't share this story, because it involved a very fearful time in my life. I had recently moved to Fort Eustis, Virginia and realized that someone was following me. Every time I left the house and returned home the phone would immediately ring and a man's voice on the other end would tell me where I'd been. He would ask if I'd gotten all of my laundry done or if I had forgotten anything at the grocery store. When I called various churches to pick me up for service he always mentioned either the name of the church van or told me the church I had attended. I didn't know who or where he was. I called the police several times but there wasn't a stalking law in effect in those days. They said unless he had done something they were powerless to help me. I tried changing my routine but it seemed that he was always watching. After a while his comments began to have an overture of threat behind them. My now ex-husband would sometimes pretend to leave to go to work, circle around and return home hoping to catch the caller. He only called when I was alone, but somehow he knew what my ex-husband was trying to do and warned me about "playing games." I was constantly looking over my shoulder not knowing whether this stalker was standing behind me in the grocery store line or face to face with me in a department store.

Finally I'd had enough, one night I took the girls, packed up and moved. When I returned home I never heard from him again.

I'm so grateful God spared me, but I wonder how many other young women have had to suffer through the mental anguish of being stalked and have had their lives invaded by such terrifying intrusions. I thank God that today there are stalking laws in effect, caller ID systems and cell phones in the hands of most Americans. All these thing were not available back in the seventies. The police are able now to apprehend stalkers under the law easier and there are severe penalties for those that perpetrate such crimes.

Chapter Ten

The Miracle of Friendship

Our next military assignment took us to Fort Eustis, Virginia. Once again I faced the task of finding a good church. I visited several before I finally found one through a friend, Lindia Batten, that I enjoyed. When I say friend, I don't use the term lightly. She was there for me during some very crucial times in my life. I was still quite an introvert when Lindia and I met, but she had the God-given ability to draw even shy, quiet individuals into conversations and make them feel good about being involved. Had the wall of shyness not been broken in my life, it would have continued to hinder me even in my ministry today. God has the right people in the right places at the right time to fulfill his purpose in our lives. Sometimes we meet people that vastly affect our lives and we call it coincidence, but there is no coincidence in God. "The steps of a good man are ordered by the Lord." (Psalms 37:23) God strategically places people in our paths to impart something into our lives that we would otherwise miss.

Often the shy, quiet, timid individual doesn't want to be secluded but finds it almost impossible to come beyond the wall that they've built up for their security. This wall is a form of bondage. The spirit of withdrawal has its root in insecurity. Inferiority causes one to think they have nothing worthwhile to contribute. It's the gateway to low self- esteem.

Feelings of inadequacy bring about feeling of loneliness and feelings of rejection. We must first acknowledge that this is not of God. It inhibits you from having free expression and proper socialization. I know, because though the Lord sent Lindia into my life and broke that stronghold, Satan often tries to rebuild the wall. But I find myself knocking down its bricks everyday of my life. It's a constant battle, but one I'm determined to win. The enemy comes to make us overly self-conscious, but I close my eyes to focus on the greater one inside, and tell myself "that greater is

He that is within me, than He that is in the world." When I preach, I talk to myself, and say I can do all things through Christ that strengthens me, and I can, because its no longer "I" but "He" that's doing the work. I fight to stay free because I know what it is to be bound. I pray that someone that's reading this story will join the fight. I'm free, free to leap and shout for joy because God sent a miracle into my life; a friend to help break through the wall of silence that has set me free in every area of my life. Don't be afraid to open the door and let people into your life. There may be a "Lindia" waiting on the other side.

Sometimes people laugh at the way I leap and praise God, but if they had gone through what I've been through, they would leap too! God set me free and whom the Son set free is free indeed. It no longer matters how anyone feels about it, my chains are broken, and I am free! Free to shout, jump up and down, run the aisle and praise my God! David celebrated till he danced right out of his clothes, Hallelujah! Paul said "I do rejoice, yea, and will rejoice!" I am through being a spectator;

I'm a participator! Don't get me wrong, the devil still laughs, he still pokes fun and tries to make me ashamed, but that's one battle I aim to win. God has given me too many victories for me to be defeated now. Jesus wasn't ashamed to die for me; I won't be ashamed to live for him. Paul said in Philippians 1:20 "According to my earnest expectation and my hope, that in nothing I shall be ashamed, but with all boldness, as always, so now also Christ shall be magnified in my body, whether it be by life or by death.

Paul said I do all things with a sincere heart and great expectancy and will not be ashamed because of my hope. Paul stood bold, confident, knowing that whether he lived or died, Christ was magnified in his body. What commitment! What intensity! If we would live every day with the zeal and passion that Paul had we would be unstoppable! We would be so big in God that men would say of us as the spies did in the land of Canaan, they would declare, "there are giants in the land."

You may be holding the key to someone's future, you may be the very one to help set another child of God free. I know I'm not the only one who stood and admired others from afar because of their freedom. You say within yourself that you desire to do this or that but you can't, you're too self-conscious. You even say "that's not me" but the truth is you wish it was you and it can be you. Don't deny yourself the freedom of praise. God wants you to be free; God wants you to be bold enough to dare. If you can't do it with your eyes open, do it with your eyes closed, but be loosed for the glory of God. It will began to affect other areas of your life that you can't see while you're bound, but get free and see. God has a blessing for you.

Be bold enough to make a friend. Proverbs 18:24 says "A man that hath friends must shew himself friendly, and there is a friend that sticketh closer than a brother." There may be someone that you've met and admired and desired to befriend but for some reason you've shied away, but that individual may be waiting on you, just as you're waiting on them. They may be saying I don't want to be a nuisance or a bother. A friend never sought is a friend never gained. Keep knocking on the door of their heart; allow God to use you to bring the miracle of friendship into someone's life. If they desire your friendship, they'll open the door. If they do, guard your relationship well, it may last a lifetime, mine will. One individual can make a difference, so go ahead, make a friend!

Chapter Eleven

I Confess

My job at the day care center only paid enough to cover my rent and the utilities. By the end of the month I was broke. I didn't want anyone to know, so I would take the girls with me when it got dark and gather soda cans and turn them in at the local grocery store.

Most of the time I bought chicken. We ate baked chicken, fried chicken, boiled chicken; we ate plenty of chicken. Sometimes we ate pancakes for dinner and the girls loved it. There were times when we didn't have enough food and I'd go without and let my children eat. There were times when I was hungry, not just having a taste for something, but hungry because there wasn't anything to eat, but my babies always had plenty. We didn't have much in those days, but David said in Psalms 37:16 that a little that a righteous man has is better than the riches of many. A man can be wicked and rich and still be poor. The little we had we blessed and we never stole from any man. God always made a way.

David said all the paths of the Lord are mercy and truth to those that keep his covenant and his testimonies (Psalm 25:10). I thank God for his mercy and his lovingkindness that was always before me. I didn't always succeed, but I tried to stay in the path of his truth that his mercy would go before me. In such unstable times I needed something that would endure forever.

After my divorce I neither dated nor entertained. I had several invitations but wasn't eager for a new relationship. I had a responsibility to my girls.

One day I was shopping and a young man asked me out. I said, "No," and soon realized he was stalking me. He proceeded to follow me as I left the downtown area. I watched in my rear view mirror as he stayed close behind. I knew I couldn't go home so I drove to the church, I knew if I could just make it to the church I'd be alright. I pulled up in front, he looked up at the church, then at me and he pulled off. I never saw him again. God delivered me from the snare of the fowler. When you don't know where to go, go to church, not everybody wants to go there!

When I came to Jesus, I didn't come to test the waters and if it got too deep, turn and go back to the shore. No, I'm not testing the waters, I'm going through the waters. If it gets too deep I'll do like Paul and his fellow prisoners at Melita. Some came on boards, some on broken pieces of the ship, but all came safe to land. I'm hanging on till I get to land!

I don't serve the Lord for the loaves, a man can perish with loaves of bread under his arms. I labor for the meat that will endure until eternal life. No matter what comes or what goes from my life I'm here to stay.

I wish I could tell you that every day I've been perfect and walked upright, that I've never fallen and never felt like quitting, but that would be a lie and I propose to tell you the truth. I confess… I've slipped, slid and fallen. I'm forty-six years old and I've had three relationships in my life. When I was eighteen years old I allowed a young couple to stay in my apartment that wasn't married. I say this to my shame. I've said things I wish I hadn't said, I've done things I wish I hadn't done, I've made bad decisions and grieved my Lord more than I can recall. I carry a sorrow that has broken my heart beyond words, an earthly sorrow that only heaven can heal, but I rejoice knowing that seeing Jesus will pay for it all. Paul summed it up by saying, "I reckon that the sufferings of this present world are not worthy to be compared with the glory that shall be revealed in us… I wait for the glory."

I make this confession, that I am the least of all his servants. I have no talent, no gift nor degree that God should desire me, but God had mercy and His grace was bestowed upon me. I labor that his grace for me won't be in vain. I confess my weakness that someone may see Christ's strength, for except "Christ be glorified." All else I've said is in vain.

One Wednesday evening I was in my backyard laying a brick sidewalk when my pastor came over accompanied by another gentleman. After a few minutes they left but the man that accompanied my pastor returned in his own vehicle.

This was our first conversation but this man began to tell me that I was going to be his wife and he was going to take care of me the rest of his life. He kept stating repeatedly, he was going to marry me. I had already concluded that he had problems and I told the girls to go in the house. They did and I locked the door.

We were attending the same church so we saw each other often. I didn't know at the time that he had asked the pastors' permission to talk to me; he wanted his blessing. You don't see that happening anymore. He asked me to go out with him. I knew I didn't want to be in a secluded place so he took the girls and I to the zoo.

Finally, one Sunday during the morning service my pastor asked this minister to come forward. He took the microphone and as he talked, an usher came down the aisle carrying flowers. I was asked to join him and my pastor handed him a ring from the pulpit. Before the whole congregation on a Sunday morning, Elder Michael T. Boyd asked me to marry him! The congregation was overwhelmed and stood to their feet and began clapping. I said, "Yes" to the man I love and we've been married for almost 17 years.

We've had our share of heartaches and pains, and if it were not for the grace and mercy of God our marriage would have been dissolved. But praise God, we're closer today than we've ever been. Often great triumph comes out of great tragedy. God can take your worst dilemma and turn it into a creative miracle. Now we can say even as Paul said, thanks be to God, which always causeth us to triumph in Christ.

We took a vow before God and all His saints, saying nothing shall separate us from the love of

God or from the love we hold one for the other. Nothing past, present or anything there is to come shall separate us. No creature, male or female, bound or free, shall separate us from the love of God or from the love we hold one for the other. We've promised to keep our vow.

God said His eyes run to and fro throughout the earth to show Himself strong on the behalf of him whose heart is perfect, (perfectly turned) toward him. I find myself throwing up my hands saying, "Here I am Lord, I volunteer, I've turned my heart toward you and if you want a demonstration model, here I am, show yourself strong in me." I want to stand perfect and complete in all the will of God and show forth the image of Him that created me. Let me fail in secularism, let me fail in philosophy, but let me not fail in Christianity. Let me not fail to win this race that I run for Christ. I run with certainty that I shall obtain the prize, and not me only, but all that live godly in this world. Those that live and look to Jesus to come shortly and redeem them from the pollutions of this world will one-day make a great escape!

We're getting out of here! This world is not our home, we're heading for that city for which Abraham searched, whose builder and maker is God. Our hope is not in this world, for all that is in the world is the lust of the flesh, the lust of the eyes and the pride of life. We've laid aside lust and put our trust in Jesus. Paul said that if in this life only we have hope in Christ, we are of all men most miserable and we're not a miserable church, we're a glorious church!

A young minister that attends our service once brought a message entitled, "Expecting the Glory." Everyday we should live expectantly, knowing that the glory of God shall be revealed through these mere vessels of clay.

At Victory Center we rejoice with joy unspeakable and full… and full of Glory! We have the victory, with no thanks to ourselves, but thanks be to God, which giveth us the victory through our Lord Jesus Christ. We don't have to work for it, we can't earn it and we surely don't deserve it, but Christ "giveth" us the victory! Praise God! Hallelujah!! We have the Victory!

Chapter Twelve

Stricken with Scoliosis

In 1982 I began having tremendous pain in my back that affected every muscle in my entire body. The pain was more severe than anything I can describe. I couldn't turn my head nor lift my arms without sending excruciating pain throughout my spine and limbs paralyzing me with pain. I suffered from severe swelling from my back through my chest cavity. The muscles around my heart were sometimes inflamed until it simulated a heart attack. I was diagnosed with scoliosis, a curvature of the spine, accompanied with osteoarthritis. One leg was longer than the other putting pressure on my hips and spine. I was told that a brace at my age wouldn't make any difference. The doctors said there is no cure and said I should abandon my job as a day care worker. They said my condition was progressively getting worse. I needed deliverance; the doctors had done all that they could do alternating between pain pills and needles. Ministers, Missionaries, Saints and friends began to pray, but still the pain was almost unbearable at times. My husband, Mike, had received orders to Italy and the doctors refused to sign my medical release because of the severity of my condition. There were no hospitals for Americans in Italy, only clinics; so unless I received healing, which would be a miracle, I would have to stay behind. We had two weeks to go and my situation seem hopeless. Then one Saturday afternoon I realized there was no more pain. Everyday for the last few months I'd woken up in pain, walked around in pain, laid down in pain and as suddenly as it came it was gone. No pain, no where! God had healed my body. He didn't send a pastor, He didn't send a missionary, but God Himself touched my body. I was free! Thank God, I was free! I decided to try out my new found freedom; I began to do sit-ups. I moved from side to side, I jumped up and turned around. I did everything but cartwheels and if I knew how to, I would have done them too! Glory to God! I had been like the woman that was bent over and could in no way lift up herself, but Jesus said, "Woman, thou art loosed from thine infirmity," and just as she was loosed and made straight and glorified God, I straighten up to glorify Him. Praise God, He is the Lord that healeth and is health to all our flesh. By the stripes of Calvary we are healed. He himself took our infirmities and bore our sickness, He will do exceedingly abundantly above all that we ask or think according to the power that worketh in us. We think it's according to the power that worketh in us. It's his power, but channeled through us as conductors of His energy. Some of us have stored energy, it's just sitting there dormant, but it's time now to bring about a release. Release the power within for the edifying of the body of Christ. Someone is waiting to be built up by that which you're sitting on. Paul called it the gift of the grace of God, the effectual working of His power, the God given ability to share the goodness of God and make it real to the hearts of men and women to draw them to repentance. If we do it to the best of our abilities, then the power of God worketh in us. If you read this book and say, "Oh, its not written well," know that I'm writing to the best of "my" ability, it may not be to your ability, but I'm giving

God the very best of my ability.

You may ask if I've ever experienced pain since that time. Yes, I have, Satan never gives up. He always come back to try my faith in the healing power of God, but I send him back with the word of God. No weapon formed against me shall prosper. He is a defeated foe and I glorify God in my body, He has made my latter days better than my former days. God has renewed my strength and I feel twenty years old and I know that's God! When I would complain about the pain in my legs, I remember the woman whom I visited that had no legs. Everyday I walk around I'm reminded of the miraculous healing power of the Almighty God. The Lord is the strength of my life; without Him I could do nothing. God is health to all my flesh, and by His stripes we are healed! I was faced with the decision as to whether to recant this testimony of healing as I felt pains run up and down my legs. The devil said to take it back for you still carry the sign and the symptoms of scoliosis, and you said you were going to tell the truth. But signs and symptoms only reflect where I've been, not where

I'm going. David saw the signs and symptoms of death but the shadow didn't make him retreat, David said "Yea, though I walk through the valley of the shadow of death, I will fear no evil, for thou art with me." So as long as Jesus is with me, I won't take it back. I know where I was, and it's so far from where I am, that it can't hinder me from where I'm going. Paul said that we as children of God are troubled on every side, yet not distressed. We are perplexed, but not in despair; persecuted, but not forsaken; cast down, but not destroyed. I was stricken with scoliosis but I've not been struck out. I have renewed hope because God's mercies are new every morning and His ways are past finding out. Who knows if He will return and leave a blessing behind Him?... and if every day with Jesus is sweeter than the day before? I can't help but step into a miracle, because everyday, Miracles Do Happen!

Chapter Thirteen

My Child Was Taken

A Mother's worst nightmare would have to be the loss of her child. It was a nightmare I found myself living. I had received custody of my three children and never thought their place with me would ever be in jeopardy. One of my daughters was finally allowed to visit her father. Everything seemed fine until I received the call saying he had her and wasn't sending her back. I'd heard of this happening to people on television but never did I imagine it would happen to me. How can I tell you the pain, the heartache and frustration I experienced as I tried to get her back? I can't count the tears I shed or the nights I laid awake living for the day I could hold my baby again. It doesn't matter if your child is thirteen, to every mother, that's still your baby. I can't began to describe the frustration of hearing her voice over the phone saying come and get me and she didn't know where she was. Unless you've lost a child you don't know the pain that rips your heart every time someone asks how many children you have. You say "three", then "two", or fixing three lunches and then remembering and having to throw one away. Imagine picking out two identical dresses for your twins and having to put one back. The babies that shared a womb for nine months are now separated for the first time in their lives and one asks when will her sister be home. No, you can't imagine, not unless you've been there. It's a nightmare no mother should ever experience, yet too many do. I know that if the Lord had not kept me day by day, giving me that daily bread, I couldn't have made it because there wasn't enough strength in me, but through Christ, I could do all things. I'm a witness that God will keep you in perfect peace if you do your part and keep your mind stayed on Him. I say this to every heartbroken mother, that if you depend on God and do your part and exercise power over your thoughts and bring every imagination to the obedience of Christ, God will be faithful and do His part. You won't have a nervous breakdown and you can keep right on praising Him even through your greatest trial. I didn't get out of the church because my child was gone. I kept right on singing in the choir, ushering on the usher board and praising God. I knew this was one time I had to draw nearer than ever before. We get it wrong, trouble comes and we run away from God, but that's the time we need to run to Him and hug Him real tight. He's the help that we need. I'd heard 2 Timothy 1:7 quoted many times… "For God hath not given us a spirit of fear, but of power, and of love, and of a sound mind." This was no time to lay down and die, this was no time to lose my mind.

If I lost my mind, how could I care for my two children I had and the one I was going to get back? I couldn't faint now, yes I cried, but I couldn't faint! I believed Paul when he said in 1 Cor 10:13 that "there hath no temptation taken you but such as is common to man, but God is faithful, who will not suffer you to be tempted above that ye are able, but will with the temptation also make a way of escape, that ye may be able to bear it." I took that to mean that my temptation, my test or trial, may measure up to my strength, but not beyond my strength. It can come to the line and test me where I am, but can't go "beyond" where I am. I know that God is able to keep that which is committed to his hands. I gave God my daughters from the time they entered the world that they too might know Him and love Him. I trained them up in the way that they should go. Too many parents tell them the way to go, but the bible didn't say, "Tell them." He said, "Train them, show them, teach them the way to go." They can never stand before God and say, "Lord, I never knew." God knows they know the way.

I thank God for my husband, Michael, who stood by me during those difficult times; he exerted every effort in his attempts to bring my daughter home. He gave of his time, energy, and finance, as my pursuit became his.

It had been a year and a half since I'd seen my daughter, but I couldn't give up now. I had to get my daughter home. Finally we had a breakthrough; a friend saw the gravity of the situation and agreed to put her on a plane. The first time it didn't work, but then I got the call I had been waiting for. She was on the airplane headed home! I received a miracle that day; God touched this woman's heart and sent my daughter home.

I'm so grateful, for I know that there are so many parents who never see the return of their child. Their search is never ending, they go on looking into the faces of every child with the same color hair or body build, hoping to find their child. Had it not been for the mercy of the God, it would have still been you or me.

God gave me a miracle, my child came home, there were some things she had forgotten and her skin was discolored, her hair no longer fell across her shoulders, but to me she was the most beautiful sight I'd ever seen! I thank God for all the years I've had with her since. I know it was a gift from God. Everyday I listen to her talking or hear her laugh, I have an inward celebration as I'm reminded that miracles do happen!

One day God will call us home and we'll

drop this house of clay and step into our eternal home. We'll gather at the marriage supper of the Lamb. None of God's sons and daughters will be missing, but we'll all be gathered home. Jesus said, "This is the will of my Father, that all which He hath given me I should lose nothing, but should raise it up again at the last day." You may have suffered loss, but be strong and be ready, and know that they shall be raised again, your child will be home!

Chapter Fourteen

Miracles in Vicenza

With the medical release now signed, I was on my way to Aviano, Italy with my husband and three girls. We stayed in the hotel for several weeks before finding a home, but when we did it was worth waiting for. It was a large cream colored house with three floors. It was very inexpensive compared to the other homes here.

There was only one gospel service in Aviano and we tried to make the best of it but to no avail. We also desired to meet more than twice a month, so we requested an alternate service. The chaplain granted our request and we met every Friday night.

One Friday a young woman stood and gave her testimony. Suddenly her eyes rolled back in her head, all you could see was the white in her eyes, her hair stood on ends. She began to shake violently. There weren't any other missionaries or church mothers there, but I knew she had a devil. I had never dealt with demons before but I found myself accompanied by two other individuals. We commanded the demon to leave. In an instant she dropped to her seat and was fine for the remainder of the service.

I was the first woman preacher at the Aviano gospel service; my first message was " Make Christ Your First Priority." We endeavored to do just that.

One afternoon I was sitting on the bleachers watching a basketball game. A young minister ran in saying that a young lady was in the chapel tearing things up and her voice sounded like a man's voice. The minister told us that the demon said to come get some of you. The minister began calling out the names of those the devil sent for. I told the young minister that I was coming. He said, "No, Sister Boyd, he didn't send for you." When I came through the chapel doors I could feel the evil presence of demons as they had infiltrated God's house. Several individuals had encircled this young woman who stood about five feet tall. She snarled and made deep throaty sounds. As I came down the aisle she grabbed the front pew and pulled it loose from the floor. I walked toward her and said, "Satan you're coming out." This strange voice said, "No I'm not, this is my house." I said, "This is God's house and you're trespassing." Satan said, "Its mine. Sometimes I sit here (pointing to the pulpit and sometimes I sit here, (pointing to the last two rows of the church)." I said, "No more, we're taking it back." I told the saints, "Let's pray."

The devil looked at the young minister and said, "Don't you pray, if you do, I'll tell on you." The young man looked at his watch and said he didn't know it was that late and he had to go. He left with two other individuals. The rest of us joined hands and began to pray, exercising the authority of the name of Jesus. The demon began to scream and about twenty minutes later this young woman sat up from the floor and began to praise God; she looked brand new and never remembered what happened to her. Praise God, she had been set free by the power of God. The name of Jesus works! Not because of who we are, but because of who He is! Joel 2:32 says, it shall come to pass, that whosoever call on the name of the Lord shall be delivered. Thank God, it has come to pass!

We went to visit the Vicenza gospel service in Italy and found out that there wasn't a pastor available to bring the word. The previous pastor had received orders and returned to the United States. The congregation had scattered but there were a few that faithfully gathered and sang songs and read the word. Elder Boyd was asked to become pastor of the Vicenza gospel service. We knew that it would call for much sacrifice on our part since the church was two hours one way from where we lived. Some pastors or hirelings are enticed to a church because of the salary. He wasn't, there was no salary, and sometimes you just have to love what you do and let that be your motive.

The distance didn't stop us from being there every Sunday, every Tuesday for noon day prayer, Wednesday night bible study, Friday night service, once a month Women's Fellowship and the

Brothers met once a month for prayer breakfast. We drove two hours one way four times a week; some people find it hard to go around the corner! We were there through the rain, snow and fog. We often drove through fog so thick we couldn't see the car directly in front of us, but God gave us traveling mercies.

We came through a maze of vehicle pile-ups on the autostrada one night after leaving the service and found ourselves parked on the shoulder knowing that it was nobody but God that put us there. I know it wasn't because of good defensive driving techniques, I was behind the wheel! My husband and three daughters were also in the van and we marveled at how cars were crashing all around us absolutely out of control because of the fog and yet God guided us safely through it all!

Psalms 18:33 "He maketh my feet like hinds feet, and setteth me upon high places."

The average American is spoiled, but we weren't spoiled in Italy. We didn't have a lot of fringe benefits over there, thank God. We only had two English speaking television channels in Aviano that we could receive. We didn't have theaters on every corner and malls down every street to occupy our time. The church bonded to become a family, Christ was everything, and we loved the church and the people of God.

We saw more people delivered from demon oppression than what I could dare tell you about. The enemy came in like a flood, but the spirit of the Lord lifted up a standard against him. There were times we thought we were going to be put out of the chapel.

Not everyone was happy about the deliverance services and often reported to the office everything we were doing, but even that worked to the glory of God. The Lord was exalted and His power was magnificent. No flesh and blood had anything to do with it. God did the work. Hundreds witnessed the awesome power of God and I've never seen anything like it since. I give God the praise, I've never met a man more worthy!!

When we took over the gospel service, there were only five members, but God began to add to the church and soon there were over two hundred and it continued to grow. The power of God fell in Vicenza and ignited a flame that will never go out. Several ministers that were working with us have since become pastors and are carrying on their work both overseas and in the United States. We saw God demonstrate His miraculous healing powers over and over again.

One Tuesday a friend brought her baby to noonday prayer saying that doctors said he needed a hernia operation. We knew God could operate on this baby and not leave a scar. We joined hands and began to rebuke that hernia and by faith in the Son of God we pronounced him healed in Jesus' name. We believed that Jesus meant just what He said in Mark 9:23 "that all things are possible to him that believeth." We believed and acted upon the word and that hernia had to go.

She took him back to the doctor and he said

he didn't need the operation after all! Glory to God! The baby was healed! I use this scripture over and over again because it works. Someone said if it works don't fix it! I don't know who said it first, but I don't work on Mark 11:24… I just believe it.

The bible says all things whatsoever ye pray and ask for believe that ye receive them and ye shall have them. Before I pray for something I make sure it's something God wants me to have. If it's healing, deliverance or things for my well being, I don't question those things because He would that I be in good health and prosper even as my soul prospers. If what I'm praying for lines up with the word of God and I can find scripture for it, then there's no reason I can't believe God for it. I just don't believe that He can or He's able; that's not faith. Faith says I believe he has even when I can't see it.

We wait to see but if we could see it then we wouldn't need to believe it. According to the word that we speak, it is done! Job 22:28 says, "Thou shalt decree a thing and it shall be established unto thee." I believe that even as we pray, the things we ask for are being ushered by faith from the realm of impossibility into the realm of possession. Faith becomes the substance, the actuality of the things asked for. God is a miracle worker, Somebody Shout Hallelujah!

While in Vicenza the power of God was so awesome until we wondered what He would do next! We saw broken bones mended, cancers thrown up, women who couldn't have babies gave birth again and again.

One Sunday morning I was making an altar call and the musician said he believed that he had a stroke. He said he woke up and his face was twisted, he couldn't control the muscles to his eye lids, he had to physically use his fingers to hold his eyes open, he was also deaf in one ear. He needed help; the stage was set for another miracle! God told Israel in Exodus 15:26 that, "I am the Lord that healeth thee." Their God was our God, He healed them, He could heal us too! He said in Proverbs 4:22 that His word is life unto those that find them and health to all their flesh. We'd found the word and He alone was our source of life. In Him we live, we moved and had our being. He is life. We began to pray and the power of God fell, I don't know at what moment this brother's eyes were opened for I was caught up in the "glory," but I heard the brother say, "Sister Boyd, my eyes, my eyes"… I opened mine and he was looking at me with both eyes opened and he wasn't holding them either, his eyes were open, Glory to God, his eyes were opened!!

The congregation began to clap their hands and praise God, but God wasn't finished yet. He still couldn't hear, but in the next moment he said, "I can hear." But it needed to be tested, the people of God were standing, without a microphone I began to say different praises and have him repeat them till finally I was on the other side of the church from him and he repeated every one. That was enough, he was hearing better than I could!! Before over a hundred people God had done it again, He had performed miracle after miracle. The old song writer said you can't make me doubt Him, I know too much about him. We don't sing that anymore, but you couldn't make the Vicenza crowd doubt that Miracles Do Happen! Praise God!!

One miracle in particular stands out in my mind that happened to my youngest daughter. She had lost a tooth in the front side of her mouth when she was six years old and it had never grown back. I took her to the dentist and was told that there wasn't a tooth in the gum, the x-rays had validated the fact. She was now thirteen and concerned about her appearance. She had grown up in the church and had witnessed the power of God many times. She came to the altar and said, "I believe God can make a tooth grow here if you pray." Now I'd never seen or heard of this being done before, but I've preached and believed all of my life that "all" things, are possible to him that believeth. Could I tell her that Mark 9:23 doesn't apply to teeth? No, the bible says "all" things. Not only that but He said He would supply all your needs according to His riches. She needed a tooth, she believed God, and if she had the faith to believe it, I had the faith to pray it! We prayed and believed God that a tooth would grow right in the front of her mouth and, Glory to God, two weeks later a tooth began to grow! Anyone that has children knows that you don't grow teeth at thirteen years old but God did it! He put a tooth where there was none and He didn't make that one any different from any of her other teeth. She has the prettiest, most even teeth you'd want to see! God did it; it was the most unusual miracle I've ever seen. God honored the faith of a young child that believed "all things are possible." She believed, and bless our God, she got a miracle, right in the front of her mouth!

One Tuesday afternoon, during noonday prayer, two police officers entered the church holding a young woman by the arm. She looked dazed and her eyes quickly darted back and forth across the room. The officer said she was sick, out of control and running in the street. He asked if we could help her. He said, "If you all can't, we'll have to commit her, but don't let her out of the building until we come back." The officer left and she started screaming and running from door to door trying to get out. Deacons and ministers stood guard at the door so she couldn't run into the street. We began to rebuke the devil that was tormenting this young woman's mind and she fell to the floor squirming and twitching, screaming to the top of her voice. We commanded the demons to come out of her and after a few moments she began coughing and clear phlegm came forth from her nose and mouth. She got up and said she had to go to the bathroom. I went with her. When she came out of the stall she had her back to me, but when she turned around she had the most perfect line of blood in both her eyes and she stood gazing at me.

I felt the evil presence of Satan as he worked his power through her. We returned to the sanctuary and proceeded with deliverance. We used Satan's tactic against him and applied the blood of Jesus. We reminded him of the blood at Calvary and how Jesus made an open show of him and defeated him before the world. He couldn't stand the blood. About an hour later she was set free to the glory of God. She never remembered the experience or how she arrived at the chapel. She left that day a new woman, saved and delivered from the oppression of the enemy. Every time I looked in the choir and saw the sweet glow on her face as she sang praises to God. She was a perfect illustration of the miraculous delivering power of God. Satan continued his assault on the people of God through affliction, depression and oppression, but Jesus raised up a mighty standard against him and set the captives free.

Too many of God's children have become victims of Satan's works. You don't have to stay bound, Jesus can and will set you free. Everyday that you remain in the state you're in, you're living beneath your privilege. Why live beneath when you can live above? Satan is getting more wicked and wiser, and just as knowledge is increasing in the earth, demon activity is also on the increase and without the power of the Holy Ghost in your life. You're no match for this wicked foe. Believe God, he can give you a miracle of deliverance.

My middle daughter, Daenel, had been diagnosed with frostbite on her legs, the doctor didn't know for sure just what to do or if in fact it was frostbite. She had severe lines of discoloration on her legs. She was concerned because it was very noticeable and asked for prayer. I remember looking at the streaks of discoloration as she walked up the aisle for prayer. As we prayed, the power of God hit her and she fell to the floor. When she got up the streaks were gone. There were no signs of any discoloration at all, she was completely healed. She was fifteen then, she's twenty-six now and it has never returned. Praise God!

One Friday night the spirit of the Lord was exceptionally high and at one point almost everyone in the building was slain by the power of God. We turned at one point in the service and saw Brother Cottingham, who was dressed in his military uniform, tilted backwards with only the rim of the heel of his boots touching the floor. I have never seen anything like it before nor since. He stood with his body completely straight, angled backwards suspended for at least five minutes on the rim of his heel. No flesh had anything to do with it. It showed God's absolute power over man. Often the spirit of the Lord would be so high in the service that no word would come forth, often the people would just begin to weep as the spirit of repentance overcame the congregation. Someone would come and bow down at the altar and soon others would follow until the altar was full of broken men and women weeping their way to Jesus.

I remember one special Sunday morning when God had truly manifested His power in our midst. People were slain in the spirit lying on the floor, still caught up in the glory of God. Deliverance and healing had been wrought in our midst and the "awe" of God was still upon us as we dismissed and prepared to leave the sanctuary. Minister Adams was standing by my van as I prepared to leave and I said to him "I don't know how I'll be able to drive these two hours home, but God is able." He looked at his watch and said, "We're a little late getting out today, but maybe you should wait a few minutes to be safe." But I decided to go on.

He got in his car and I got into the van and backed out. I remember going forward in the parking lot and seeing several things go past as though in a fast forward speed; but to this day, I don't remember driving. Two of my daughters were in the vehicle with me and they also said they don't remember the ride home but they witnessed the fact that we traveled a two hour distance in the space of thirty minutes. Shontel, my oldest, kept saying that she know she wasn't sleep, she was awake the whole time, it wasn't a dream. She explained how she saw scenes going past as we traveled and within a half hour we were in our driveway.

To this day I can't tell you how we got there. We immediately went into the house and checked the television channel guide because they always had the right time. It was one of the most mind-boggling miracles I've ever witnessed. We were transported forward by God at a time when I found it almost impossible to drive because of such a residue of God's anointing.

It reminds me of the story of the Ethiopian Eunuch who was sitting in his chariot reading

Esaias. Phillip came and opened up the scripture to him and baptized him and the spirit of the Lord caught Phillip up. The eunuch didn't find him any more, but Phillip was found preaching at Azotus. I believe that's the same thing that happened to us in that van. I have no other explanation except for God's supernatural intervention that carried us so swiftly from one place to another. God does work in the miraculous, believe it or not… Miracles Do Happen!

About six years ago on a Sunday morning, I had finished our morning radio broadcast and was on my way to church. On that particular morning I talked about "The Wiles of the Devil." I decided to make a quick stop at the vacant mall to get a soda. I dropped my change into the machine and heard a car speeding through the parking lot in my direction.

Now I always park in between the white lines, but since the lot was empty I parked across the lines. I didn't know that in a few moments that simple act would be to my advantage. I turned to look at an approaching car. Two men jumped out and one remained standing by the car as the other came toward me. I saw the driver lean his front seat forward and I knew I was in trouble. As the man nearest me reached out I went toward my car and as I did the other man yelled, "Get her, get her." I looked and in an instant both men were frozen in place! The passenger of the car was so close to me that he could have easily grabbed me, but for a reason I can't explain, he froze and I quickly got into my car. His hand immediately reached for my door handle; I slid the lock and drove off.

Had I parked any differently that day I would have been trapped between the sidewalk and the man's car. Had I cut my car off I may not have had time to get my keys and put them in the ignition and drive off. If any one circumstance had been altered, I wouldn't be here today to tell my story.

If it had not been for the Lord watching out for me that day, the enemy would have overwhelmed me and taken me captive. I don't know if they froze because they saw something or froze because God simply stopped them in their tracks. All I know is they stood perfectly still until I was inside my car.

When I left they didn't follow me. I went straight to the church. I praise God for his goodness toward me, how He has saved me over and over again. David said " Oh, that men would praise God for His goodness and His wonderful works toward the children of men." God's hand of mercy was upon me and He was my refuge in a time of trouble. He defended me when I had no defense and made a way of escape. When my enemies' thoughts toward me were evil, God blessed me before their face!

Peter said in 2 Peter 2:9 " The Lord knoweth how to deliver the godly out of temptation, and to reserve the unjust unto the day of judgment to be punished." The Lord is a strong deliverer and will raise up whatsoever standard is necessary to deliver those that love Him. God will deliver the just, but there is a day of reckoning for those that do evil and teach others to do the same. God is angry at the wicked everyday and every nation that forgets God will be turned into hell.

They that need Him shall not be forgotten. The expectation of the poor shall not perish but it shall come to pass. Often we expect too little and receive the little that we expect. David said God shall give us an expected end. I expect to be blessed, I expect God to come through for me. I expect Him to deliver me when I get in trouble. My God said, "He's able to do exceeding abundantly above all we ask or think according to the power that worketh in us." We should expect no less than to receive that which is above all that we can think or imagine, that we may be filled with all the fullness of God.

God rescued me when I would have otherwise perished. The devil meant it for evil, but God turned it to my good, that in everything He be glorified. There is an incomparable value to our trials. James said, "Count it all joy when ye fall into divers temptations (trials), knowing this, that the trying of your faith worketh patience."

The end result of our trials is to add unto our lives until we're perfect and entire, wanting or lacking nothing. Every trial should make us more complete in Christ, bringing another level of anointing into our lives.

I've seen a woman, who was wheelchair bound for years, get up and walk, Mother Mormon hadn't walked for years, and I was bringing the word one Friday night when the spirit said, "Tell her to get up and walk around the church." I did and continued on with the message. Immediately she got up and walked around the church and up the middle aisle. Everyone started clapping and praising God. I thought that they were really getting into the message, I hadn't paid any attention to the fact that she was in a wheelchair, but when I looked at Mother Mormon she was crying. I stopped and asked her what was wrong, she said "I haven't walked in years, but I just walked around the church and up this aisle." She kept on walking and giving praise to God, she walked right into a miracle!

I've had the opportunity to be in Rome and read the book of Romans. I've been into the inner prison and seen the stocks and chains that once held Paul captive. I've seen the Cistine Chapel where the famous paintings of Michelangelo are exhibited. I've been to Venice where the body of St. Mark is entombed and seen the leaning tower of Pisa. I've seen Florence and other cities throughout Italy. I've been to Switzerland; to Paris, France and seen the Eifel tower.

There is only one thing left that I desire of the Lord, and in the words of David, that will I seek after, that I may dwell in the house of the Lord all the days of my life, to behold the beauty of the Lord and to inquire in His temple.

My soul will then be satisfied for I've preached the gospel on every permissible corner and witnessed to every ear that will hear… I've told the world that miracles do happen!

Chapter Fifteen

Thank You Lord

I want to thank you Lord … I really do. But how can mere words thank you for giving me life? How can words express the gratitude I feel for all the times you've been there for me and never left me? How do I thank you for sanity? How do I do that? Words seem so insignificant, so futile, but oh God!… how I thank you, I worship you. I love you more than anything. I'll thank you for the rest of my life!

Thank you Lord for not letting me be ashamed of my testimony, for the glory of God has been revealed through it all, and wherever the glory is, there can be no shame. Paul said in 2 Timothy 1:12, "I suffer these things but nevertheless, I am not ashamed, for I know whom I have believed, and am persuaded that He is able to keep that which is committed unto Him against that day."

Lord, if this be the trial of my faith, I pray I have tested well.

My faith has not stood in the wisdom of men but in the glorious power of God. To Him be glory!

I've written this book with many tears, it has caused me to remember so much. Thank you, Lord, for my trials, for it was good for me to be afflicted. With my head lifted up I can now declare that my trials are secondary to what I've found in you!

Thank you Lord.

Chapter Sixteen

He's Not Finished Yet

I realize that all of our trials and afflictions are designed for one purpose and that is to conform us to the image of Christ. The fact that we could be worked on to such a degree, that we could have any resemblance to Christ is in itself miraculous! This was the pre-ordained plan and wisdom of God. It was predestined that we who ran, wrestled and agonized our way to the foot of the cross would one-day rise up and sit in heavenly places in Christ Jesus, we'll sit with the anointed one!

The Lord is calling us to get further away from where we've been in order to get closer to where we're going. Many of us are destined to partake of some miracles that we may declare the glory of God and tell somebody that miracles do happen! God desires to lead us into purpose and the more we lay aside our own goals and focus upon God's agenda until our agenda becomes

God's and God's becomes ours and there is no difference one from the other, then we'll find ourselves moving into purpose. If we can finally arrive at the place where we began to do as Paul said and die daily, we'll find that as we die, more of Him can live. That's what John was talking about when He said, "I must decrease that He may increase." The miracle of our union with Christ is that we die, we decrease that the righteousness of the law of God might be fulfilled in us. Roman 8: 4-5 says we walk not after the flesh, but after the spirit. For they that are after the flesh do mind the things of the flesh, but they that are after the spirit do the things of the spirit. We struggle to remain the same, not concerned with conforming but keeping our own image. Commercials have told us that image is everything but image is not everything, Christ is everything , in Him we live, we move and have our being.

Many individuals are trying to find ways to pump up their bodies and develop strong bones that we can be healthier, look better and live longer. But we often forget that we are what we embrace.

If we partake of fatty foods the results will show up on our scales. If we live recklessly our lives have the potential to end drastically. If we embrace carnal things then carnality is reflected. But if we embrace Christ, then Christ is reflected in our lives, we become the embodiment of Christ!

It's awesome to know that we have the presence of Christ, the anointed one, the brightness of God's glory and the shining forth of His presence in us. In Hebrews 1:3 Paul called Him the brightness of His glory and the express image of His person. The true revelation of His presence that He proposes to release into our lives is miraculous but few ever attain this depth in Christ. But as surely as I know He lives, God desires to reveal His glory in the lives of every born again believer. But its up to us how much of His presence we allow to radiate through us.

Christ in us is a miracle from God, the question is, what will we do with Him? Will we keep Him as a souvenir of our salvation? Or will we allow Him to arise within us and be The Mighty

God, The All-Sufficient One, and God in Christ and Christ in us? Jesus is the word revealed, and the word mingled with faith dipped in expectation will bring about glory in our lives. Often we hope but we don't expect a move of God. The woman with the issue of blood knew that if she could just touch the hem of His garment, she would be made whole, she expected to be healed. We must expect to be set free, healed and delivered, we must expect the glory!

The more we abide in Christ, the more He abides in us. The closer we get to Him, the more He shows up in us. Whatever a man has on the inside will be released on the outside. If there's nothing on the inside, there won't be anything on the outside.

The attributes of God's glory in us is faith, honesty, knowledge, truth, temperance, patience, godliness, kindness and the remaining fruit of the spirit listed in Galatians 5:22. If we are in Christ and Christ is in us, what comes out of us should be Christ. The mirror only reflects the image before it. We are the mirrors that reflect the image of Christ. It's not our image that needs to be glorified, we must do as John the Baptist said, " I must decrease that He may increase." Our spirit man expands according to the knowledge that we have in Him. It's not book knowledge, it's not head knowledge, but it's heart knowledge!

Many know of Him but only a remnant know Him. Paul said, "That I might know Him, and the power of His resurrection, and the fellowship of His sufferings, being made conformable unto His death."

Paul knew Christ, he didn't just know of Him through the written word, but He knew the living word. Paul knew the power of Christ and it affected his life so traumatically that he was forever changed, he didn't know the old man Saul anymore, he had moved so far from where he was that he could only glory in where he was going.

Paul knew he was on his way to see the King. Paul touched the power that brought Christ to life again and declared, "Now I know the power of His resurrection!" We must die to sin in the same way that Christ died for sin. Our trials bring us closer and closer to Christ until finally we're close enough to fellowship with Him. As we're molded and shaped into form we take on the image of Him that shaped us, we die and Christ lives in us.

2 Peter 1:3 says, "Grace and peace be multiplied unto you according as His divine power hath given unto us all things that pertain unto life and godliness, through the knowledge of Him that has called us to glory and virtue." Grace and peace was multiplied upon the New Testament believers and extended to you and I.

It didn't come by the will of man but by the divine power of almighty God. He that freely gave us His only Son has given us all things that pertain unto life and godliness. I see a miracle in there! Everything to sustain our lives and everything to keep us godly is in Christ, the Anointed One, and the anointing destroys the yoke that comes to kill, steal and destroy in our lives. Satan's yoke is destroyed because of the anointing!

God has called us to glory and to virtue. It wasn't men going after a glimpse of God's glory, it was God calling men to glory and He wanted it to work for us. God wants His glory to be revealed in our lives. 2 Peter 1:4 says, "He has given unto us exceeding great and precious promises that we might be partakers of His divine nature." His glory has always showed up in degrees in our lives. His glory showed up one night while the shepherds were in the field watching over their flocks by night and the angel of the Lord came and there was glory all around them.

Exodus 14:19 tells the story of the angel of God that went before the camp of Israel. The pillar of cloud came before their faces, then moved and stood up in the back of them. It must be wonderful to have the glory of God before and behind you!

When Moses talked with God in Mt. Sinai his face caught a reflection of God's glory from being in His presence. Moses' face shone so with the glory of God that he had to put a veil over it. I wonder how many of us have had to veil our face recently?

I thank God so much for His plan of salvation and that He included me. He could have left me out. I didn't have any gift or talent to offer Him. I had absolutely nothing to give but while on others He was calling, He didn't pass me by. I thank God He included me in His plan. Paul said in Ephesians 1:4, "God hath chosen us in Christ before the foundation of the world, that we should be holy and without blame before Him in love, having predestinated us unto the adoption of children by Jesus Christ."

It was nothing less than a miracle of love that the Father showered down upon us. God knew we didn't deserve His favor and yet He went beyond favor and loved us who were unlovable, made holy those that were unholy and took away the blame from those that stood before Him guilty on every charge. When mama and daddy put us down the Lord our God took us up and adopted us as His children and now we are the Sons of God. Glory Hallelujah! What kind of love is this! John didn't understand it either and said " Behold, what manner of love the Father hath bestowed upon us, that we should be called the Sons of God."

God's miraculous plan of bringing glory into our lives through the breaking of our vessels is not only mysterious, but also undeniably brilliant. We resist being broken because we want to avoid pain, suffering and any forms of discomfort, but the breaking of God is not to destroy us, but to conform us to be more like Him. God has placed the light of His Son within us and unless we become broken, the light will never shine through. In Judges 7:13-20 Gideon came against the Midianites. He took three companies of one hundred men and told them to hold glass pitchers in their left hands with lamps on the inside of the pitchers.

They held their trumpets in their right hands and together they shouted the sword of the Lord and the sword of Gideon. Three hundred men broke their glass pitchers and the light on the inside showed through in the darkness and their enemies were confused and began to kill one another. Just as those men broke their vessels and let the light shine, we must break our vessels and let the glorious light of the Son of God shine from our hearts. Often we shy away and won't open up and tell others about Christ.

Break the silence, let the truth be told. The devil doesn't know what to do with the light, He becomes confused every time. Open up and let the light shine! If we let it shine it will illuminate those around us. We have a precious gift inside, we have inherited glory, passed on from God in Christ to Christ in us, Jesus has it without measure and we have it with measure.

The only difference is that we don't know it. We don't know the totality of the power within us. We're not powerless beat down rag muffins. Our elder brother defeated the devil, conquered death, hell and the grave, rose with all power in His hand, gave us the victory and said, "Now you're more than conquerors." Jesus is our Lord, God is our Father and we are the Sons of God!

Ephesians 1:11 says we all have obtained the same inheritance, predestined according to the purpose and counsel of God's own will. The same inheritance Christ has in Him, we have in us.

God wants to bring about some glory in our lives, even in our mortal flesh. Paul said, "the life also of Jesus might be made manifest in our mortal flesh." Our trials work in our mortal bodies for the express purpose of making us strong and out of great strength comes great victory. God wants to do some unveiling. He wants to show off the glory that's on the backside of our mountains. We're operating with unrealized power, but even now, I feel a glimpse of glory is coming!

We must make a shift in our attention from ourselves unto God and know "whose" we are. We must stay sanctified and not compromise. David said we must know that the Lord has set apart the godly for Himself. We must be available for service. Often we get busy with kingdom business and don't have time for the king. Kathryn Kuhlman said it well, "God's not looking for golden vessels, He's not looking for silver vessels, He's looking for yielded vessels." We must be available.

The church must live expectantly. Live as though you're on the verge of a miracle, expect the glory, look with expectant faith, and expect to be blessed, expect to see the glory!

If the veil that blinds our eyes is ever lifted and the glory of God is revealed in our lives, and the church, the body of Christ, rises to full power and renounces the hidden things of dishonesty, not walking in their own craftiness, nor handling the word of God deceitfully and realizes the treasure shut up in these earthen vessels we would turn the whole world right side up.

But we're moving closer. The cross is going to get heavier, it's getting us ready for the crown.

Joel's army (Joel 2:28) is on the rise, we're coming out, we're rising with expectant faith and the glory of God shall overshadow our lives "and it shall come to pass in the last days saith God, I will pour out of my spirit upon all flesh, and your sons and daughters shall prophesy, and your young men shall see visions and your old men shall dream dreams and on my servants and my hand maidens I will pour out in those days of my spirit and they shall prophesy and that's glory, that's glory revealed!

Conclusion

Sometimes we go through the storm of life and ask "why me, Lord?" But perhaps we should ask, "why not me, Lord?" Shall we receive good only at the hand of the Lord?… No, it's the balance in life that builds true character.

Some soldiers go to battle and just lay down in the trenches and hope for the best, but Gods' not looking for trench diggers nor lazy recruits, neither is He handing out medals to those suffering from battle fatigue. God is looking for those men and women that will endure hardness as a good soldier. God wants a few good men and women to enlist in this army and fight the good fight of faith and remain courageous till they lay hold on eternal life. Paul said in Romans 5:3 that we glory in tribulation, but many of us wait to glory "after " tribulations. Our tribulations will improve our patience and give us experience pertaining to the things of God. Through much patience and sufferings we become a living testimony read of men and from cover to cover I declare this testimony is true…

Miracles Do Happen!!